Animals and Us

GUARD Animals

By E. C. Andrews

BEARPORT PUBLISHING

Minneapolis, Minnesota

Credits
All images are courtesy of Shutterstock.com, unless otherwise specified. With thanks to Getty Images, Thinkstock Photo, and iStockphoto. Recurring – Nezakat Kerimova 71. Cover – Roger de la Harpe. TOC - smrm1977. 4–5 – RudiErnst, Erica Hollingshead. 6–7 – olgagorovenko, Andyworks. 8–9 – Michelle D. Milliman, Denisa V. 10–11 – Olga Aniven, Jaromir Chalabala. 12–13 – C. Hamilton, Noe Besso. 14–15 – cctm, Fred Cardoso. 16–17 – alisie_b_, Jukka Jantunen, Volker Heide. 18–19 – KarinR, Microscope, Дина Попова. 20–21 – Germanroam, YesPhotographers, Dmitri Maruta. 22–23 – Oleggg, Luca Fabbian.

Bearport Publishing Company Product Development Team
Publisher: Jen Jenson; Director of Product Development: Spencer Brinker; Managing Editor: Allison Juda; Editor: Cole Nelson; Associate Editor: Naomi Reich; Associate Editor: Tiana Tran; Art Director: Colin O'Dea; Designer: Kim Jones; Designer: Kayla Eggert; Product Development Specialist: Owen Hamlin

Library of Congress Cataloging-in-Publication Data is available at www.loc.gov or upon request from the publisher.

ISBN: 979-8-89232-730-5 (hardcover)
ISBN: 979-8-89232-780-0 (paperback)
ISBN: 979-8-89232-817-3 (ebook)

For more information, write to Bearport Publishing, 5357 Penn Avenue South, Minneapolis, MN 55419.

Contents

WHAT ARE Guard Animals?

Working animals help us in a lot of ways. Some of them watch over and **protect** our homes and farms. These creatures are called guard animals.

Other types of working animals include support and police animals.

There are many different kinds of guard animals. These special workers look out for **threats**. Their job is to keep dangerous people and hungry **predators** from getting into places they should not be.

Guard animals can help make us feel safe.

A Special KIND OF Animal

It takes a special kind of animal to be a good guard. They must be brave. A guard animal also has to be **loyal** to their owner. These two things help build trust between a **handler** and the animal.

Being able to sense danger is part of a guard animal's job.

An animal helper must always pay attention to their surroundings. It is important that they are not distracted by the things around them.

GUARD Dogs

Some guard dogs are trained to protect homes and families. They bark to tell their owners when someone is nearby. This loud noise also scares away threats.

Guard dogs are often found in front of the home or business they are protecting.

Other guard dogs watch over **livestock**, such as sheep, goats, and chickens. These animal helpers chase away predators that try to get close to farm animals.

Livestock guard dogs keep farm animals safe from coyotes and foxes.

One of the most important lessons a guard dog must learn is how to follow commands. Being a good listener helps them work well with their owners.

Handlers can teach animals to understand words and hand signs.

Guard dogs are trained to bark and show their teeth when they see a threat. This is done to **communicate** with their handler that there is danger. They will attack only if the threat does not go away.

GUARD Llamas

Llamas (LAH-muhs) can make good guard animals for goats and sheep. These special workers stay near the **herd** they are protecting. Llamas have eyes on the sides of their heads. This helps them watch over the whole herd at once.

Llamas protect livestock from coyotes and wild dogs.

Guard llamas have cool ways of defending their herds and themselves. They scream, kick, and even spit at any predators that get too close!

Llamas can spit up to 10 feet (3 m).

Training guard llamas starts when they are young. Before they turn three years old, these animal helpers are put with the livestock they will protect. This lets the llamas begin to **bond** with the other animals.

Llamas eat the same food as the livestock they watch. They all munch on grass and hay.

All llamas kept as pets or working animals are trained with a halter. Owners can use halters to lead llamas where they need the animals to go.

A halter is a type of collar that goes around a llama's head.

GUARD EMUS

Emus are big birds with excellent vision and hearing. They can run up to 30 miles per hour (48 kph). That makes them great at chasing away threats.

An emu claw

Emus fight against predators by stomping on them.

Along with being fast, guard emus are also very strong. They have long legs with sharp claws on their feet. An emu kick can cause a lot of harm.

GUARD Donkeys

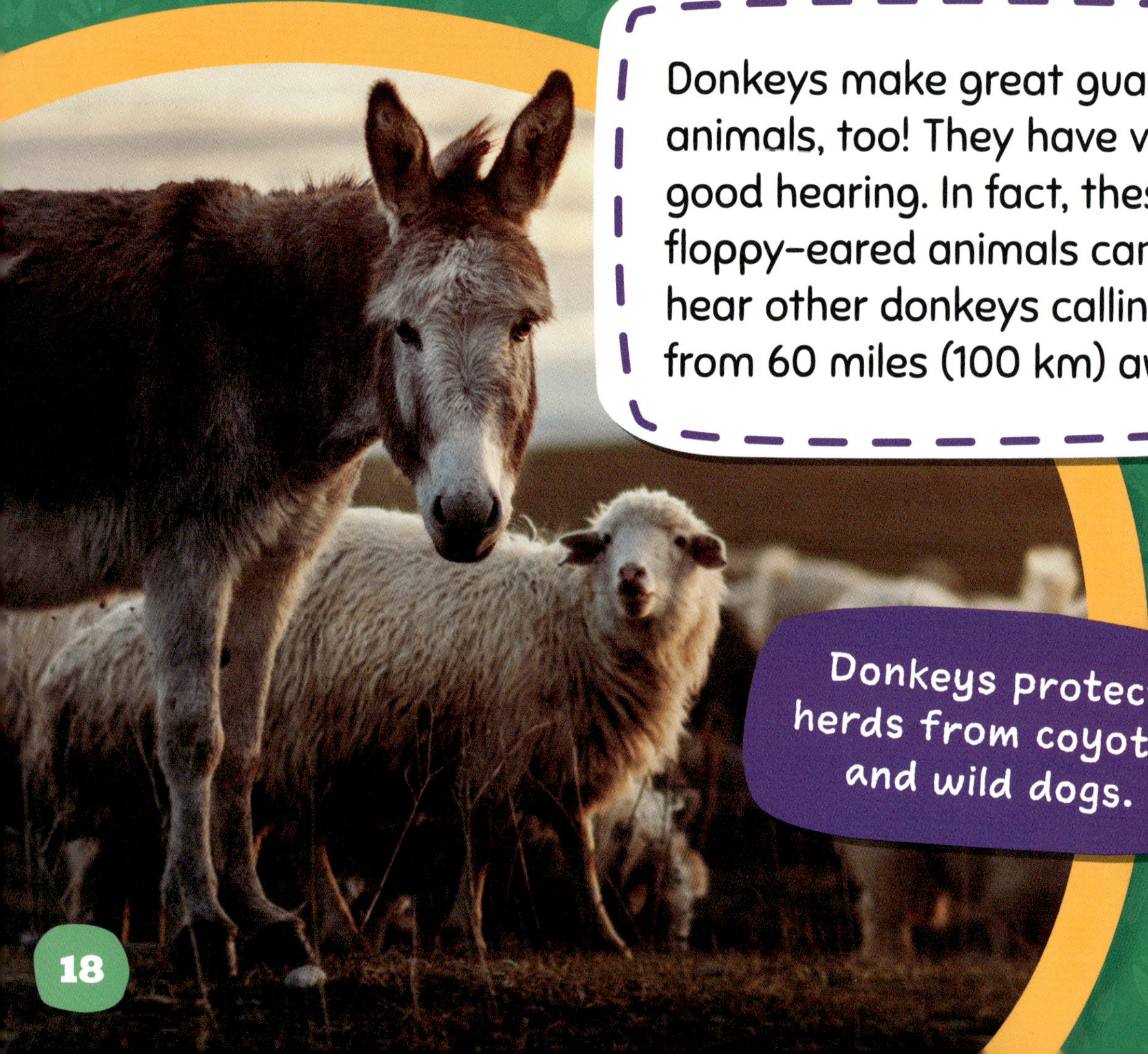

Donkeys make great guard animals, too! They have very good hearing. In fact, these floppy-eared animals can hear other donkeys calling from 60 miles (100 km) away.

Donkeys protect herds from coyotes and wild dogs.

Sometimes, donkeys make loud noises to scare away predators. This is called braying. Braying lets the herd and their owners know about danger.

A donkey braying

Donkeys may bite and kick predators to keep them away.

GUARD Geese

Geese may be small compared to other guard animals, but they are just as mighty! They are not scared of big predators. This makes geese a good choice for keeping land and farms safe.

Geese live and work together. They take turns eating and keeping a lookout.

A goose honking

It is best to have two geese to protect a place.

These helpful birds are loyal to the people and other animals they grow up with. They have a loud yell called a honk. When danger is near, guard geese will honk to let their owners know.

Guard Animals AND US

There are many kinds of guard animals that help us in different ways. They play an important role in keeping us safe, solving problems, and making our lives easier.

Handlers should give their animals plenty of food and water.

Always treat working animals with love and respect. Taking good care of these animals helps them stay strong, happy, and healthy while they work.

Glossary

bond to form a close friendship or connection

communicate to share thoughts, ideas, or information

handler a person who trains and works with animals

herd a large group of the same kind of animal

livestock animals, such as cows and sheep, that are raised by people on farms or ranches

loyal faithful to others

predators animals that hunt other animals for food

protect to keep something safe

threats things that could cause harm

Index